The Simple Keys to a Happy Relationship

Geary Reid

ISBN: 978-976-8305-70-1

Acknowledgments

Great thanks must be expressed to the following people:

The heavenly Father, for granting me the wisdom and inspiration to record the information in this book, which I began on November 17, 2021, and completed on November 20, 2021; my family, for their continued encouragement and support regarding various challenges; and several people who have assisted with reviewing and editing the book:

- Hance Theodore, CIA, ACCA
- Chalsea Amanda Lewis, LLB, Diploma in Communication Studies, Diploma in Project Management
- Joyce Sullivan
- John A.S. Clowes, MSc., BSc., Dipl

To you, the reader: have fun while reading, and grasp and practice what you learn so that this world will become a better place. Many people are depending on your guidance. We all need a shoulder to lean on and a hand to guide us.

Geary Reid
MBA, FCCA, FAAPM, MPM, CAT

Reid's Learning Institute and Business Consultancy

reidnlearn.com

Amazon: amazon.com/author/gearyreid

Facebook: Reid n Learn

Instagram: Reid n Learn

LinkedIn: Reid's Learning Institute
and Business Consultancy

199 Kuru - Kururu, Soesdyke Linden Highway
Guyana, South America

Table of Contents

Introduction

Couples who are in love know that they are allowed to show affection towards each other, long before they are in closed chambers. Their love must be an ever-expanding and constantly evolving cycle. Those in relationships must seize every moment to let their partner know how much they appreciate them.

There are many things that couples can do to express their emotions without saying a word. These non-verbal expressions will cause partners to feel attracted to each other. Couples do not have to wait until they are in a private place to express romantic feelings for each other. When couples hold hands in a gentle manner, it often sends a message that only they can interpret and respond to. Eye contact can also put persons in a good mood to connect with their partner.

Oral and physical hygiene is important for romance. Those who constantly practice good oral and physical hygiene may recognize that their companions often want to be in their presence, even if no words are said.

Both partners must monitor their diet and place much emphasis on exercising. Eating healthy meals and exercising are very important for persons to stay in shape and ensure that they remain attractive to their companions. The seductive clothes that some persons want to wear to capture their partner's interest require them to make some adjustments in their diet and exercise in order to get their body in shape and cause their partner to constantly admire them. Dancing together will help couples to keep fit and also add to their romance.

Persons must avoid spending too much time on their phones and computers when their companions are with them. They must try and complete most of their business as early as possible so that they can allocate more time to look at and listen to their companions. Those who work very hard to accomplish many things for themselves and their families must give some time to their partners, since they are still expected to be romantic as they acquire important things for their families.

This literature is divided into four important and practical sections. The last section is devoted to relaxation and investments. When couples choose the right places for their vacations, they may add more value to their relationships. Every couple must be willing to invest time and money in each other's lives, and they will watch their relationship grow.

Attending the theater and watching movies together allows couples to relax and also learn many ways to improve their romantic relationships. If couples participate in sports, they will have more time to work as a team, disagree with each other, and then once again agree to work together as a family. Birthdays and wedding anniversary celebrations are two major events that some couples place much emphasis on. When the bed and bedroom are attractive to them, couples will want to spend more time there with each other.

Section A. Non-verbal communication

The success of many relationships is not always dependent upon the words uttered, but on the non-verbal communication between partners. Non-verbal communication in relationships is powerful and will often make one partner respond in a way that is anticipated by the other partner. When one partner stretches out their hands, the other partner may quickly stretch their hands for a hug. The gentle touch of one partner may cause many great things to happen in the relationship.

Many times, persons learn the messages sent by their partner's eye contact. They do not have to attend a university to know what some types of eye contacts mean. Eye contact may indicate yes or no, so each person must read their partner's expression and decide what course of action to take.

Oral and physical hygiene are two things couples must practice daily. When they keep themselves clean, they may spend more time together than apart. Bathing frequently and using cologne can set the stage for romance. If couples can afford it, they should each purchase fragrances that will cause their partner to be attracted to them.

A smile by one companion can be a great thing that their partner expects to see. Some smiles may turn into laughter when couples are comfortable with each other.

Styling of the hair and haircuts can also add to the romantic life of couples. For wives, there are many hair accessories that they can use in order to appear more romantic.

Talking is very good for all relationships, but persons in a relationship sometimes need to be quiet. In their silence, they will internalize what their partner is saying. A romantic relationship does not require one partner to be a journalist, but sometimes just requires both partners to be quiet and enjoy each other's presence.

1. Eye contact

When persons are in relationships, they learn that eye contact can be a very powerful communicator, as it can communicate either "yes" or "no" to the other partner. Someone may say little, but what the eyes communicate may be greater than what they can express in words. Use eye contact effectively and the relationship can be great.

As the relationship grows, sometimes there is less need for words, as each partner can send and receive messages through eye contact. A staring look with a serious face may imply "danger" or "no," while a smiling face and a gentle look may be saying "yes" or indicate that the other person is in agreement.

Many persons may recall that they started a conversation with their current partner because of eye contact. For example, both of them were sitting at the same table, and they looked at each other. At some point, one person may ask the other person, "Why are you looking at me?" and the other may reply, "I don't know, but why are you also looking at me?" Based upon that interest, they will communicate during or after the fellowship at the table. This may be the beginning of their relationship, because each person wants to know why the other one showed interest in them.

Many children will be able to assess their parents' mood by looking at their eyes and body language. If children sense that their parents are in a good mood, then they will approach them. However, if their parents appear not to be in a good mood, then the children will stay away from them.

When persons are in relationships, eye contact can be like a magnet that draws their companion's interest and attention towards them. However, when they are angry with each other, those same eyes will send a message to the other person to keep their distance.

When couples are constantly avoiding eye contact, even when they are alone, it may be a sign of danger that something is wrong in the relationship. It may be only a matter of time before external persons start to recognize that those couples who do not have regular eye contact may be having problems.

Even when couples are having lunch or dinner, they can make eye contact with each other as they sit at the same table. Some persons are too busy working for their employer or doing domestic activities that they do not get much time to sit with their partners. However, couples should set aside time to eat together, and that may create opportunities for them to look at each other as a form of expressing their emotion. For those companions who are working, many times when they return home and look at the eyes of their partners, they can assess if it is going to be a good evening or a bad one. If it is a bad evening, then each person may keep their distance, but if the evening looks good, then it may be time for togetherness.

2. Touch

Touch is another type of non-verbal communication that is used in a relationship. When a couple has great chemistry, a gentle touch from one partner may be more than the words either of them could say, and no fire tender can put out this fire of love.

When a sick child is taken in the arms of their parents, that touch may work like medicine, as the child may soon recover. Sometimes, children believe that their parents are doctors because they do certain things that result in those children feeling better.

2.1 Harsh touch

Oftentimes, a harsh touch creates unease in the mind of one partner. They can become upset with their partner whenever this is done. Most times, when partners have lived together for some years, they will learn that a harsh touch may be greeted with unpleasant words or eye contact indicating to the other partner that their touch was not welcome.

2.2 Warm hand

Touching your partner with a cold hand can often cause discomfort or negative feedback, but the touch from a warm hand may be relaxing and provide comfort. When partners are relaxed, they often have opportunities to think of good things, and this may work towards the advantage of the other partner.

2.3 Gentle touch

Gentle touching in a relationship is often important to convey a message to a partner. When couples have disagreements, a gentle touch may be of no value, and a stranger touching another person gently may not have much effect. However, if one partner touches the other gently, it can mean so much.

If partners return home from work and have a bath and something to eat, along with a gentle touch from their partner, they may forget about the stresses of the workplace, because their partner's touch gives them a sense of comfort. This gentle touch may give them energy to return to work and make a significant contribution for their employers.

2.4 Hugging

While hugging and touch are different, they have some similarities, as they both require the effort of one partner to reach out to the other physically. Both of these activities can be done without a word being said, and they can both cause the receiving partner to feel loved.

While workmates and friends will hug each other, a hug between partners is different. There is no restriction on how often partners can hug each other. It should be done frequently, as it is a way of communicating among partners.

2.5 Shoulder to lean on

Most times, when we think of a shoulder to lean on, we think of it figuratively. But literally allowing your partner to lean on your shoulder, especially after they have had a long day, may build intimacy and romance. Lending one's shoulder may look different among couples because of height differences, but the effect of emotional support remains the same.

3. Holding hands

Oftentimes, partners walk together and hold each other's hands. This is another important thing for couples to do. When it is done, each person in the relationship may feel secure and know that their partner loves them.

3.1 Gentle hand-holding

The holding of hands among couples must be a gentle act, not done with great might. Oftentimes, if a man holds his companion's hands too firmly, she may show signs of discomfort or communicate to him that he should hold her hands more gently. Yet if they are in danger and one partner has to provide protection and support to the other, then the firm holding of hands may be acceptable.

3.2 Evoke positive feelings

The holding of hands often evokes positive feelings among partners. They may do this very frequently, as they know that they each look forward to the positive energy that flows through both partners. Holding hands may be supported by hugs, eye contact, and kisses.

When some couples go anywhere, they are often walking together and holding each other's hands. They do not grow tired of doing this, because they are communicating with each other. However, if it is seen that partners are frequently avoiding holding each other's hands, it may be something to consider. They may be having challenges in their relationship that causes them not to want to connect with each other.

Couples can sit and hold hands, or they can do it while they are walking together. Some may be envious of those partners who frequently hold hands, but they should convert their energy away from envy and start practicing holding their partner's hands more frequently.

3.3 Give it a try

Couples who are not accustomed to holding hands frequently should start practicing at home. Once they become comfortable with holding hands at home, then they can practice it at other places until they are no longer afraid to hold hands in public.

Not every couple will be seen holding hands, and it does not mean that they are not in love. They way that some persons were trained by their parents may cause them not to want to hold hands with persons, including their partner. However, they may find other ways of expressing their non-verbal communication with their partner.

Children sometimes know when their parents are not having a good relationship of communicating with each other. Therefore, partners must work towards quickly reconciling their differences and loving each other. They can go for a walk, talk about their differences, and then begin to hold hands again. It may be difficult to hold hands again after having a disagreement, but it may show maturity that both partners are willing to forgive each other and make up their relationship. The longer couples take to reconcile their differences, the more pressure they put on their relationship, and the relationship may soon come to an end.

3.4 Times to avoid holding hands as a couple

Some couples hold hands when they are driving, but this practice must not be encouraged, since the driver needs to keep both hands on the steering wheel. When couples are attending to their children or cooking, they should avoid holding hands, as they will be required to provide undivided attention that may require the frequent use of both hands. Once couples are finished with these activities, then they can resume holding each other's hands.

4. Bathing

Bathing quickly is one thing, but having a bath that makes someone clean is another. For some persons, bathing once a day may be acceptable to them, but others will bathe two or three times each day. Bathing is important to do, and each human must cultivate this habit. This means that must not wait to decide to bathe until they are going to some event. When a person is single, they must learn the importance of personal hygiene. They must know that bathing is not optional, but something that is essential and must be done daily.

Figure 1. Frequency of bathing for persons in a relationship

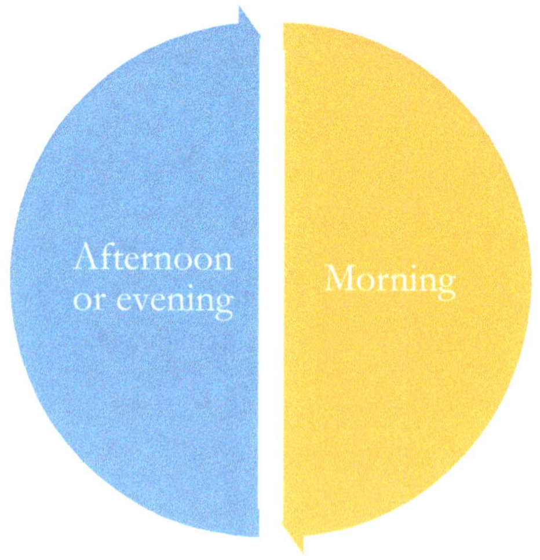

(All figures developed by the author unless otherwise noted.)

Bathing at least twice per day allows each partner to remove any odor from their body. The human body will sweat or give off some odor, regardless of how much cologne a person may apply to their skin or clothing.

It is a good habit for some persons to take a bath when they awake, before they prepare their breakfast or get involved in any major activities.

Persons who are depressed may feel great after having a bath. While all of their stress may not go away, they may feel a renewed sense of relaxation.

Figure 2. Why must couples bathe frequently?

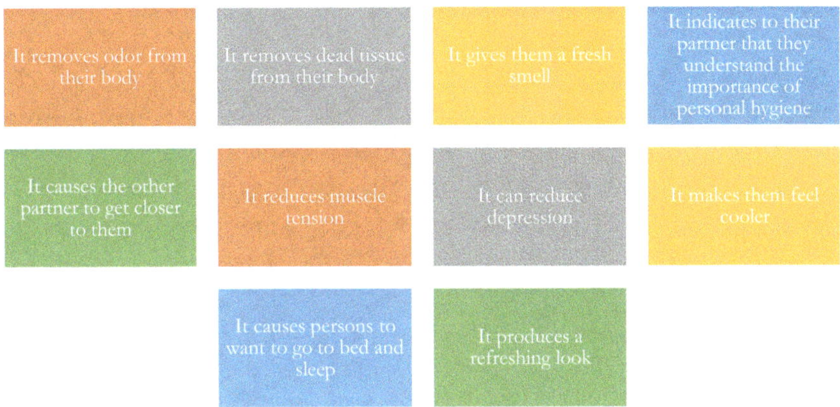

Those who sweat frequently may choose to bathe very often. Once some persons are finished with their major activities in the afternoon, then they will take a shower and get ready to have a relaxing evening with their companion.

4.1 Warm bath

When a person has a warm bath, they allow their body to be relaxed. The muscles sometimes need this good treatment. A warm bath also helps to heal wounds.

Within some homes, persons may not have the option for a warm bath from their shower. However, there are several other options that they can utilize to have a warm bath.

When the outside temperature is hot, persons may not want a warm bath, as it will cause them to perspire excessively. However, if the outside temperature is cool, then a warm bath will be most appropriate.

4.2 Bathtubs

Persons who have enough space within their homes may install bathtubs. For those who are currently constructing their homes, they may want to consider installing a bathtub if they have enough funds to purchase one. In the bathtub, many persons will spend time allowing most of their bodies to be submerged in water. Many persons will add fragrances to the water in the bathtub, which gives them a refreshing and good smell after they have finished bathing.

Persons who are preparing to go to work may not have enough time to spend in the bathtub. However, if they have time and do not have to bathe quickly, then they may enjoy some time in the bathtub.

After a bath, persons may feel very refreshed. They may feel energized to get many things done, or they may feel like getting in bed to go to sleep.

5. Oral hygiene

Everyone in a relationship expects their partner to know the importance of oral hygiene and to practice it daily. It can be very disturbing if one partner does not practice proper oral hygiene, but expects their companion to be comfortable with them.

Figure 3. Frequency of oral hygiene

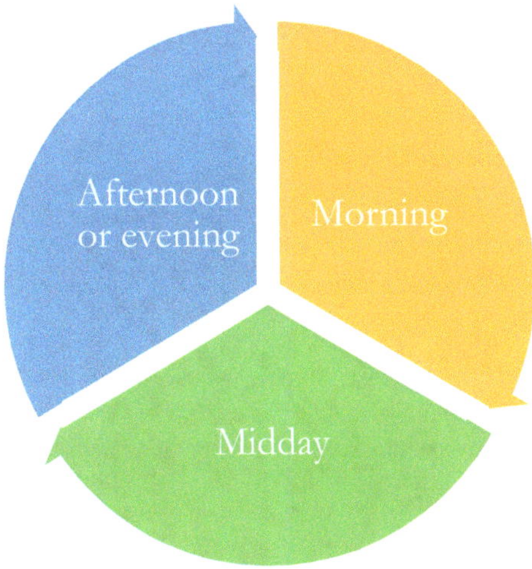

Many parents will train their children to practice regular oral hygiene, telling them to brush their teeth in the morning, after lunch, and before they go to bed. The message that parents want their children to learn is that oral hygiene is important and must be done frequently. Some parents will tell their children to brush their teeth after every meal. Proper oral hygiene prevents tooth decay and removes odor from the mouth. Besides brushing of the teeth, persons must also brush their tongue, and this must also be done daily.

5.1 Visit the dentist

Everyone needs to visit the dentist. These visits are not always for the extraction of a tooth, but to get the dentist's feedback about their oral hygiene. Many persons will visit their dentist once or twice a year. There are some persons who have hardly ever visited a dentist, but it is something important for them to consider. No one should wait until they are experiencing oral health challenges before they visit their dentist, as frequent visits may prevent them from developing certain common oral health issues.

5.2 Things that are important for maintaining daily oral hygiene

Many persons choose to eat whatever they want. However, they must take responsibility for maintaining good oral hygiene, not only for the benefit of others, but also for their own benefit.

Figure 4. Things that are important for maintaining daily oral hygiene

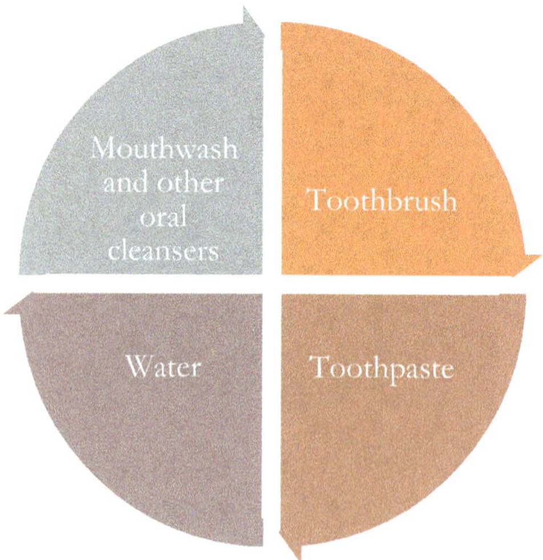

Each of the four items mentioned in the illustration above has a great impact on oral hygiene.

Toothbrush. Use for brushing the teeth and tongue. There may be some solid sediments stuck between the teeth that are not removed when a person gargles liquid in their mouth.

Toothpaste. This will be placed on the toothbrush and will be used to brush the teeth. The toothpaste will remove or kill germs that are in the mouth. Some brands of toothpaste are more effective than others.

Water. It is important to use water during and after brushing of the teeth, as it helps to remove all solid sediments inside the mouth. Persons are encouraged to rinse their mouth properly during and after brushing of their teeth and tongue.

Mouthwash and other oral cleansers. There are times when the toothbrush will not be able to reach every small place in a person's mouth. Sometimes, solid sediments may be stuck in parts of the mouth and the toothbrush will not be able to remove them. However, mouthwash and other oral cleansers will remove these sediments and also allow a person's mouth to have an attractive smell.

Some couples have special oral care products that they like. Therefore, whenever they visit the market, supermarket, or pharmacy, they will purchase their favorite oral hygiene products. Some families will only use certain brands of oral hygiene products, and they do not plan to change to a different brand.

When it comes to oral hygiene, persons must not compromise on this important area of their lives, since if they neglect it, they may lose many friends and probably their companion.

Some persons will brush their teeth, and after washing out their mouth, they will use mouthwash. Those who are employed may not have the opportunity to brush their teeth while they are at work, but they may be able to use mouthwash to cleanse their mouth and allow their breath to be acceptable to members of the public.

When persons know that their breath is fresh and free of odor, then they are confident in speaking to others. Those who are in relationships will be willing to speak very close to their companion without second-guessing themselves about their oral hygiene.

6. Colognes and fragrances

One of the senses that humans were created with is the sense of smell. When something does not smell pleasing to their nostrils, they will ask about the smell or stay far from wherever the smell is emanating from. However, if the scent is pleasing, it will cause many persons to get closer to enjoy the sweet smell of the fragrance.

When a person uses certain colognes or fragrances, they often cause persons to be more willing to allow them to come closer. In most relationships, when each partners has on cologne that their companion likes, it creates an atmosphere where one partner will inhale the beautiful scent and feel comfortable in their partner's presence.

Remember, when couples are at home, it may allow them to enjoy each other's presence. When the fragrance is right, it will cause both persons to be relaxed and want to spend more time with each other.

6.1 Fragrances for work

Most persons will ensure that they have cologne and deodorant, and they will apply these fragrances to themselves before they leave home to go to work. When persons have enough money, they may purchase different deodorants and colognes specifically to be worn at work. Some employees will also apply cologne before they leave work to go home. This may be very important for those who have to use public transportation after engaging in much physical activity at their workplaces, which causes them to perspire enough that their body odor has changed.

6.2 Fragrances for other places and events

Persons may have different colognes for going to school, sports, religious events, etc. Once again, this may be optional, if they have the ability to purchase multiple colognes. Some persons like to create different impressions in the minds of people when they are at different places and activities.

6.3 Fragrances for home

Each couple can decide on the fragrances that they would like to use at home. For some persons, this may be an expensive thing to do. However, attracting their companion by having on a good-scented cologne at home will be very good for their relationship. Too many times, persons do not want to invest in their relationship, and when their companion is no longer in their lives, then they think of things that they could have done, including spending more money to recapture their former companion's heart.

Some couples may not have enough funds to purchase different fragrances for different places, and that is understood, as it is optional. However, if they can afford it, it is something to consider . It is important for couples to have an attractive smell when they are home as well, since they will be spending time with the one they love so dearly. Persons sometimes invest in having various fragrances while at home, since they want to create a different feeling in that personal environment. While they are the same person at home, their scent may cause their companion to love them more and more.

7. Haircuts and hairstyling

The way some persons cut or style their hair can make a great impression on the minds of others. For men, cutting or trimming their hair may not be costly, but it is often more expensive for women. Some wives will go to the barbershop with their husband and wait until he finishes having his hair cut. From the barbershop, they will go to have something to eat or drink. Some men will also go to the salon with their wives when she has to get her hair done. Often, because of the time it may take for women's hair to be styled, they may let their companion go and do something else in the meantime, then call their companion to collect them from the salon when they are finished.

7.1 Barbershop and haircuts for men

Most men will have regular barbershops that they attend. They may go there frequently, as they feel comfortable with their barbers. Men are often happy when they go to the same barbershop and the same barber is there to give them haircuts that they are comfortable with. Because the barbers are familiar with cutting and styling these men's hair, they do not have to give the barbers any guidance, since the barbers know what to do.

As some men grow older, they may change the style of their haircut. Due to nature and aging, some men will have less hair on their heads, so they may eventually become comfortable with having a bald head. There are other men who will try different products to cause hair to grow on their heads, especially if they are losing a lot of hair.

Not all men like to look like their age, so some may choose to dye their hair as they age. For men who want to look younger, different haircuts and styles may enhance their looks and may also enhance their relationship with their companion.

Shaving of the beard is another thing that many men will do at the barbershop. Each week, most men will shave their beard so that they look acceptable to others, and it may be part of the requirements for the organization they work for.

7.2 Salon and haircuts for women

Many women enjoy going to the salon to get a refining hair makeover. This sometimes gives them a whole new look, making them more willing to approach the public with great confidence. Many husbands are happy to go places with their wives and to hear how good she looks. There are some men who constantly take care of the expense for their wives' hairstyle, as they see it as a worthwhile investment in the person they have chosen.

Women have so many ways of making their hair look impressive and appealing to their companion. For example, they may cut their hair, add artificial hair to their natural hair, color their hair, etc. There is so much that women can do with their hair that will cause them to look royal.

When women are getting married or attending major events, birthdays, wedding anniversaries, and other important occasions, they often look forward to a hairstyle that will speak volumes about them. It may be expensive to maintain many of these hairstyles, but women may choose to do this to enhance their look.

Beyond the hairstyle, there are many fashionable things that women can place on their heads to enhance their look, such as head wraps, beads, hairpins, etc. Many of these little things that women will add to their hair may make them look different to the public and continue to make their companion feel proud of them.

8. Smiling

Smiling is another type of non-verbal communication that is important for every couple. There is a time to be serious, but there is also a time to smile. Some persons seem to have to learn to smile. Due to the struggles of life, they may have become so serious that they rarely smile.

Persons who are involved in law enforcement and military institutions may have to be serious for most of their day. School teachers may also have to be serious daily while they teach students. However, a relationship is very different from a person's work, so when persons are with their companions, then they must smile. They do not want to make their companion feel like they are still at work.

When persons choose not to smile, they cause tension in their face muscles. However, if they choose to smile, they give themselves more reasons to relax and live a healthy life. Smiling must not be done to please others, but it must become a lifestyle for many persons.

8.1 Attract persons

Those who often smile may recognize that they attract persons to themselves. Sometimes, they may attract persons who will not add any value to their lives. However, most persons will like to be around those who smile and are comfortable with themselves. They may not be bothered when those persons are serious at times, because they know that it is the norm for those persons to spend more time smiling than being serious.

Smiling and laughing are two different things. When persons are having a good time, they may smile and laugh, and when they are finished, they feel relaxed, as they have enjoyed themselves.

8.2 Smiling opens doors for conversation

Smiling opens doors for healthy family conversation. Many times, both partners may talk more if they sense that their companion is relaxed. As they talk and smile, they may find themselves discussing many things, including things that are very strategic for the relationship.

On many occasions, when one companion looks at the other's face and sees a serious expression, they sense that it may not be the most appropriate time for certain conversations. Some companions will know that their partner had a busy and stressful day at work just by looking at their partner's face. The smile they are accustomed to seeing is no longer there, and their partner appears to be sad, distracted, or focused on something else.

When some persons find a companion, they move from being very serious to very jovial. They tend to be happier with others, and instead of hardly communicating, they are more open to various conversations.

Children sometimes quickly assess their parents' non-verbal communication. If they see their parents with serious faces, they will not approach their parents. However, parents who smile and appear to be relaxed will often find that their children will approach them frequently and ask many questions.

Parents can still decline their children's requests with a smiling face. However, most parents often try to be serious to indicate to their children that they do not agree with what was asked. When many children grow up and become parents, they adopt a similar approach, choosing not to smile when someone requests something from them that they do not plan to give.

Figure 5. Things couples can do to cause themselves to laugh and smile

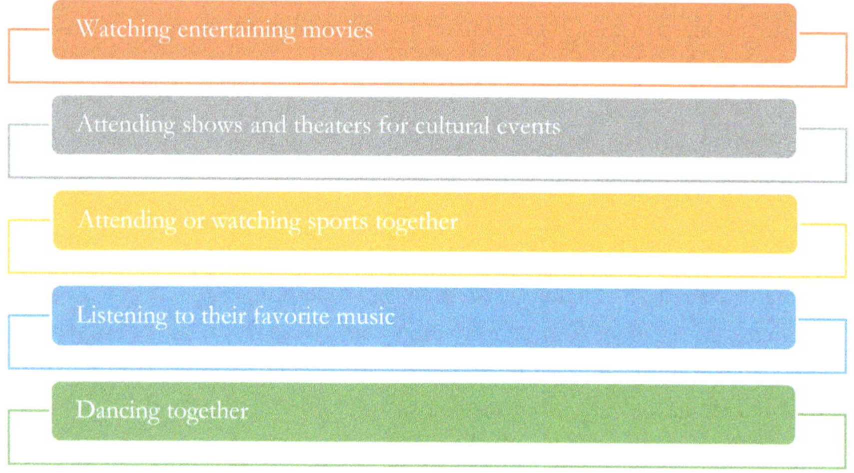

8.2.1 Watching entertaining movies

Couples may choose to watch movies together. As they watch, they may see something hilarious that will cause them to smile and laugh. Some adults will watch comedies by themselves, with their companion, or as a whole family. As they watch these comedies, there may be much laughter. Some persons may laugh until tears come from their eyes, and they feel satisfied because they have found a way of relaxing.

Horror movies and news may cause the opposite effect, as those who watch may become fearful or very serious. There are some persons who are selective with the news that they read or listen to, since they know that certain news items will disturb them.

8.2.2 Attending shows and theaters for cultural events

Many couples go to shows and cultural events because they want to have a relaxing time. Some couples work very hard and try to have a work/life balance. When they attend these events, they get time to laugh at themselves and laugh with others.

There are some shows that are designed to make persons laugh, such as stand-up comedy and nights of poetry. Even at karaoke, there may be much laughter. It is a worthwhile investment to spend money on entertainment that gives you the opportunity to laugh, rather than spend money at the doctor to fix stress-related matters.

8.2.3 Attending or watching sports together

Couples may set aside time to attend sports together. As they watch the players, there may be reason to laugh at what happens. Watching sports may be done from the comfort of one's homes, and they may see something while watching that causes them to laugh. On weekends, some persons will set aside time to attend or watch sports, as they need to find something that will make them smile and laugh.

8.2.4 Listening to their favorite music

Not everyone likes to dance. However, many persons will listen to their favorite songs. They may sing along with the songs and they may smile at the lyrics. Some songs cause persons to reflect on their past or find energy to see possibilities in their difficult moments.

8.2.5 Dancing together

Couples do not always need plenty of space to dance. They can dance in their dining room, in their kitchen, or even in their bedroom. Sometimes, while they are dancing, one partner may do or say something that causes the other to smile or laugh.

There is so much fun that couples can have if they choose to enjoy themselves. The more time couples spend enjoying themselves, less space they leave for stress and disagreements.

9. Be quiet and listen

There are some partners who feel that they are journalists who must report on all issues. It is very good to speak about many issues, but there are times to just be quiet and listen.

Romance does not always require much talking. Sometimes, looking into each other's eyes may be good enough to send the right message to a companion. There is a time for plenty of talking in a relationship, and there are other times to be quiet.

When persons are mentally drained, they may not want to hear much noise. They may not want to hear the voices of others, including that of their companion. When persons are quiet, they get the time to relax and be rejuvenated for the next assignment.

Couples who understand each other may learn when to leave their partner alone. For some couples, when they see their partner return home from work or school and go straight to bed, they get the message to leave their partner alone. There are other times when one partner will come home with a sad countenance, and this may be a good indicator that something is bothering them. After living with each other for some time, some non-verbal messages are very clear.

When parents want quiet time, they can instruct their children to be quiet. Children often understand this message and will find somewhere else to play where they do not disturb their parents' peace.

When persons are fully rested, then they are ready to spend time with their partners and children and talk about how they can build their relationship. For some couples, a quiet moment may be like medicine for them, as it eases their stress.

A good listener has to learn to be silent. They cannot talk while the other person is talking. As one person stays quiet, they also give themselves time to think, and they show that they respect the other person's views.

Being silent allows persons to reflect on life. In those quiet moments, some persons are able to reflect on their own relationship and be thankful for the progress it has made.

There are some persons who need a quiet atmosphere in their household. When some persons want quiet, they may choose a vacation destination where they do not have to answer telephone calls or be visited by many persons.

Section B. Physical activities

In a couple, each person expects that their partner may treat them to good meals. Some couples will spend time dining at home or at the places they prefer. As they dine together, they have time to look at each other and express their appreciation to each other.

Some couples like to dance. As they dance and feel the gentle hands of their companion, it may stir their sensuality.

Keeping in shape is something that every couple must do. This may require them to attend a gym or purchase gym equipment. With regular exercise, each person may get the body shape that attracts their companion.

The clothing worn by persons can be appealing to their companion. Therefore, they must know their companion's taste and what clothes will cause their companion to feel the need for closeness. The clothes persons wear to work will be different from the clothes they will wear in the bedroom.

10. Diet and cooking

Persons who want to enhance their relationship must carefully consider their diet. When persons overeat, they do great harm to their health. If they choose to consume foods that are low in nutritional content, then they will also be doing harm to themselves.

Parents must teach their children to eat healthy meals. As a result, many of them will live healthy lives when they become adults, which will continue even when they are in a relationship. Sadly, some persons have to spend much money on their health because they failed to pay enough attention to it at an early stage.

It is important to be aware of the nutritional terms in the table below. While some of them are spoken of regularly, they are not always properly understood.

Table 1. Food and nutrition terms

Food and nutrition word	Explanation
Diet	The food that a person eats typically every day. There are also special diets, e.g., slimming diets, low-fat diets.
Malnutrition	An incorrect or unbalanced intake of nutrients.
Under-nutrition	An insufficient total intake of nutrients.

Balanced diet	A diet that provides the correct amount of nutrients for an individual's needs.
Nutrition	The study of nutrients and their relationship with food and living things.
Nutrients	The molecules in the food that the body uses to function correctly and stay healthy.

(Extract from Tull & Coward, 2009)

Each person in a relationship must try to preserve the health of their companion. In some families, their medical bills use up most of the money they earn.

10.1 Preparing healthy meals

Both husbands and wives must be conscious about their health. When they have to prepare meals or purchase food items, they must read the nutritional contents of the items they are about to purchase or prepare.

In the home, many parents know that their children will have a few favorite meals and may not want to eat other meals that are prepared. However, parents must work along with their children to ensure that they are getting a balanced diet. The meals for children and adults must contain most, if not all of the main groups of nutrients identified below.

Table 2. There are five main groups of nutrients

Main groups of nutrients	Explanation	Sources of the nutrients
Protein	The primary function of protein is to provide body-building or growth materials, so every cell in the body contains proteins.	Meat, fish, cheese, eggs, wheat, rice, oats, beans

Fat (and oil)	Provides a convenient and concentrated source of energy, supplying more energy than the same weight of carbohydrate or protein.	Meat, butter, margarine, fish, nuts, fruits
Carbohydrate	Carbohydrates are the most important source of energy for the body. Almost all the cells of the body use glucose to distribute energy. Carbohydrate acts as a "protein sparer" so that protein can be used for its primary functions rather than as a source of energy.	Sugar, honey, molasses, jam, jelly, yam, sweet potato, breadfruit, rice, barley, corn
Vitamins	Vitamins are a group of chemical substances, most of which were identified during the 20th century as vital to the body. The body requires only small amounts of each vitamin. Vitamins can be classified according to the substances in which they dissolve.	Milk, cheese, eggs, carrot, spinach, watercress, cabbage, tomato, pumpkin, Callao, cod liver oil

Minerals	Bodybuilding. Control of bodily processes. Essential parts of body fluid. Some mineral elements are required in relatively large amounts.	Milk, cheese, broccoli, bok choy, legumes, bread

(Extract from Tull and Coward, 2009)

Most times, the meals that parents prepare for their children are the same ones they will eat themselves. Therefore, every parent must prepare meals that allow the family to be healthy by containing nutrients from the various food groups.

10.2 Preparation of meals

In some relationships, both partners know to cook, and that is always a good thing. However, there are other relationships where only one partner knows how to prepare meals properly, and that can put a strain on the other person. Nevertheless, in the name of love, the partner who does not know to cook can make some sacrifices and learn this skill.

Teaching an adult in a relationship to cook may not be easy as a parent teaching a child to cook; nevertheless, everyone who has a partner must be willing to invest time in helping that person to become better. This teaching can start out with simple things that will make them familiar with the kitchen, keeping the kitchen clean, and finding items within the kitchen.

If someone is not skilled in cooking and wants to be more helpful within the kitchen, their partner might start with some of the following activities:
- Having them clean the kitchen surfaces
- Having them wash the dirty utensils
- Letting them light the stove or oven
- Letting them wash and cut up the vegetables
- Letting them measure and assemble some of the ingredients that have to be used for the preparation of the meal
- Having them clean, cut up, and season the meat
- Letting them stir and progressively check the meal that is on the stove or in the oven
- When the meal is finished, letting them serve each family member

These responsibilities must not be given to them all at once. Remember that the intention is to get them to learn to properly prepare meals and begin to enjoy this new and important family activity. After trying for some time, they will become familiar with it, and therefore, they will ease the burden of the other partner who was often in the kitchen preparing meals. As both persons are in the kitchen, there will be many opportunities to discuss many things. Each person has the opportunity to look the other in the eyes and express appreciation for them.

Some couples will play music while they are preparing meals, which can give them the opportunity to sing and dance while they complete these activities. The kitchen can be a place where couples have the opportunity to build on their relationships without having to set aside more time to communicate and show their affection toward each other.

If the new chef has done a good job in cooking, then something must be done to compliment or reward him or her. Just as little children like to know that they have done something good and look forward to validation, a similar thing can be done for the companion who is now learning to cook. A hug and kiss may be some physical ways of showing appreciation for their effort.

11. Dining

Couples must make time for dining. While they may often be busy, they must sit down and eat together. When persons eat and drink together, they have the opportunity for so many conversations. Each person can also look the other one in the eye as they talk and eat.

11.1 Dining at home

Couples can arrange their homes and dine right there. They can set up the place in a manner that creates a romantic atmosphere for them. Even if the house is small and their possessions are limited, they can have an enjoyable time at home. They can adjust the lights in the house to give the effect that they need, and they can have a candlelit dinner right within their own home. They will choose the music they will listen to and the beverages they will consume.

Figure 6. Advantages for couples dining at home

<table>
<tr><td>There is no need to allocate time for traveling from home to another location</td><td>No transportation or fuel cost will be incurred</td><td>No need to have a babysitter to attend to children while the couple is out of the house</td></tr>
<tr><td>The couple will eat and drink as much as they want without incurring additional costs</td><td>Items purchased to create a romantic atmosphere can be reused for another occasion</td><td>No need to hire security to watch over the house in the absence of the couple</td></tr>
<tr><td></td><td>All conversation shared at home remains with the couple</td><td></td></tr>
</table>

11.2 Dining away from home

Some couples prefer to dine away from home, which is also acceptable. They may want to go to a special place and enjoy the romantic ambiance, rather than being in the same place they are accustomed to.

There are times when some places will have special events and arrangements for couples to dine out. Each year, there may be special events where couples can spend time dining out. For example, Valentine's Day is an important date for many couples to go out for a meal. Couples celebrating their birthday or anniversary may look for someplace different to visit, so they may choose to dine away from home.

Figure 7. Advantages for couples dining away from home

Even those who are not working for large sums of money must take time to invest in their romantic relationship. They must work deliberately to build that relationship, since they do not wish to leave space for intruders.

At some external dining places, couples may have the option to dine inside the building, or perhaps within an open space or one that allows them to see many natural things, like trees and flowering plants. Sometimes, persons can eat alongside the pool. Not many persons are able to have their own pool, but this option may be available at an external dining facility.

With outdoor dining, persons have the opportunity to look up into the skies and see the moon and the stars. The temperature may be most appropriate for couples to dine outside. There are some persons who spend much of their time in air-conditioned offices and long to enjoy the natural environment. The clothes worn by some women will make them feel more comfortable with the outdoor temperature, rather than the cool air from the air-conditioning unit.

Some couples may want to taste a variety of beverages when they are dining. Therefore, dining away from home will give them the option to choose whatever beverages they want, and they may only have to pay for the quantity that they consume. With the right food, beverages, and atmosphere, it may be good for couples who want to be romantic.

12. Dancing

Dancing is something that stirs much emotions in couples. Even if a couple wants to dine at home and play songs, they may not have enough space to dance. When the music is right, persons need plenty of space to dance and enjoy themselves in the safe arms of their partners. Neither of them need to be professional dancers, but they dance to have fun, and indeed they do.

Figure 8. Why couples should dance together

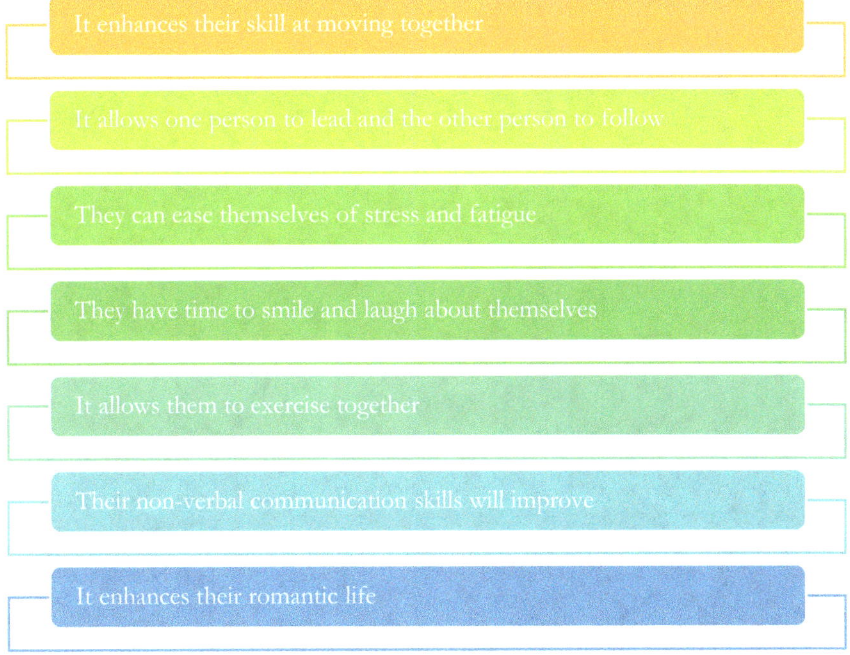

In some homes, couples will dance together most weekends. They will choose the songs they like and keep dancing until they are tired. Once they are tired, they may eat and then begin dancing again.

Couples who are good at dancing may participate in dancing competitions for couples. At those events, they may showcase their skills and be rewarded.

When some couples have had enough practice dancing together at home, then they may go to another place where they can dine together and then dance. They may also invite other couples within the family circle to their home, and they will play some songs and dance. This may be a time of great fun and getting to know each other.

13. Clothing

Oftentimes, the clothes people wear can be a major attraction to others. Before some couples came together, it was the clothing that sparked one person's interest in their future companion. The clothes that persons wear do not always have to be the shortest or closest-fitting to attract another person, but sometimes the mixture of color and how the clothes fit that person may be the winning combination.

It is not always the brand and cost of clothes that makes them appealing, but it may be the person wearing the clothing who causes all eyes to look at them. Therefore, no matter what clothing you wear, you have an opportunity to make it look good on you.

13.1 Caring for clothes

It is important that both persons in a relationship care for their clothes. They are expected to get their clothes washed frequently and properly stored away until the next time they wear them. The area where these clothes are stored may have some sweet-smelling air freshener to give the clothes a good smell when they have to be worn. In caring for their clothes, persons must ensure that they use detergents that will help to preserve the color of their clothes.

13.2 Clothing accessories

Sometimes, bags, belts, necklaces, watches, sunglasses, stockings, leggings, suspenders, and other accessories may enhance the appearance of a person. Many persons may choose certain clothing accessories that will make them stand out when they attend public events. There are some accessories that can match a variety of outfits and will not need to be changed when different pieces of clothing are worn.

13.3 Clothes for home

The clothes that persons wear at home can also be a reflection of who they are. So, when they are in a relationship, they must wear clothes that will cause their partner to appreciate their effort to be properly attired.

13.4 Clothes for work

Some persons may have a standard style of clothing for work. Many organizations will issue uniforms to employees, or they may indicate the styles of clothing that are acceptable for the work environment. Those who want to keep their jobs will comply with the dress code of the organization.

Persons who are working in factories, machine shops, and other places may have to wear protective clothing, and staff who are attending to customers may have to wear specific uniforms issued to them by their employers. Customer service representatives are often required to wear something that indicates their names so that customers can properly communicate with them.

13.5 Clothes for social and cultural events

Most couples will have certain cultural, religious, and sports events that they will attend. The clothes they wear to these events will be different from what they wear at home. So, couples may have different clothes for particular events. There are some couples who will purchase similar outfits or clothes in matching colors. When there are cultural events, there will be complementary clothing for a husband and wife to wear. If a couple chooses to purchase matching clothes, they can create a look-alike effect, which can make them unique in the public eye and proud of each other privately.

13.6 Clothes for the bedroom

The clothes some couples buy to wear in their bedrooms may be more expensive than the clothes they buy to wear at work. This may be because, if they fail to capture their partner's attention, they may make their partner vulnerable to other persons.

A relationship is often a work in progress, since nothing is ever complete or perfect. After many years, the clothes someone has worn in the bedroom to entice their companion may have to change as each person grows older. Nevertheless, each person must begin to assess their companion and know what clothing works best for them in the bedroom. If the bedroom attire is not appropriate to their companion, it can affect the couple's romantic life.

The human eyes are attracted to what they see. So, in a relationship, clothes can be a motivator or a demotivator. It is always important for you to keep your companion attracted to you, rather than strangers.

14. Exercising and keeping the body attractive

When persons are young, the volume of activities they are involved in may keep them fit and healthy. However, when they grow older, they may have to exercise to keep themselves healthy.

People sometimes see exercising as a difficult thing, but it may not be too difficult if they choose to engage in simple exercises. Many persons may complain that they do not have time to exercise, but if they properly manage most of their activities, then they will have enough time to engage in exercise.

While not everyone may be able to visit a gym, some persons can walk within their communities, go cycling in the park, or clean up the leaves in their yard. These simple activities will enable many persons to get themselves in shape.

Sometimes, exercising and body building will give persons a different physical appearance, which can make partners more attracted to each other. When many persons first started their relationship, they might not have been in the best of shape, but as they continue, they may receive advice from their partner on things they can do to improve themselves. One such thing is to exercise and be in good shape.

When persons exercise, they will reduce extra fat and tone their physical structure, which may cause their partner be more excited to see their body. Some couples will go to the gym together in order to motivate each other. When they go together, they will use the same vehicle, which will minimize transportation costs. On their way to and from the gym, they have more time to talk and laugh with each other.

Setting up a home gym may benefit both partners, as they can exercise or get their bodies in shape in the comfort of their home. Some couples may hire personal gym instructors or body-building trainers to work with them from their homes, perhaps several days each week. This routine exercise may cause both persons to get into shape quickly.

Consuming healthy food is always important for persons who want to keep themselves in shape. They must minimize fatty foods and foods that are high in carbohydrates. The quantity of food eaten in the evening may be something that couples will have to monitor. Therefore, whichever partner is responsible for preparing dinner will have to make some adjustments to include foods that are more nutritious to the body. The person who is responsible for shopping for groceries and other food items will have to include more fruits and vegetables for those in their families who wish to eat specific meals.

If persons are not disciplined with their diets, they may not reduce excess fat and may not get into shape as they had planned. However, if they are disciplined with their diet and exercise, then they will be in shape and make their relationship very romantic.

Section C. Things to avoid

There are certain things that couples must avoid. For example, persons should not have many lengthy telephone conversations when they are with their partner. Couples must set aside time for each other, since time is a great investment that will build a relationship. When a partner sees his or her companion making time for them, it may draw them closer to each other.

Couples who are too busy with work and friends will not have enough time to build their relationships. While persons would like to accomplish many things, they must not put their accomplishments above the time they need to spend with their companion.

Busyness robs companions of time to spend with each other. Couples who have children must teach their children early to help with domestic activities in order to reduce their parents' workload, thus allowing the parents to spend more time building their romantic life.

15. Manage your phone conversations

The phone is a good device for communication. With so many things happening, people need the ability to be informed or pass information from one person to another. Schooling is now often done through mobile devices, as students can submit their assignments via their phones and learning institutions often communicate with students electronically. Business transactions are done using phones, so it would be very difficult to remove phones from the lives of people.

After persons meet for the first time and show an interest in each other, many of their conversations may take place on the phone. For those couples who are living in different countries, the phone will be an important communication device for them to remain connected.

15.1 Minimize lengthy conversations

Once couples establish a relationship, they must spend time with each other. They will still have friends and families and workmates, but it is important that they minimize their conversations with external persons and give more time to their companion. Especially at the early stage of the relationship, both persons will need to spend more time talking in order to get to know each other.

15.2 Put your phone on silent

When couples are going on lunch dates, it is important that they both put their mobile phones on silent, snooze, or some other option that allows them to give their undivided attention to their companion. When couples are at home, they may also have to practice putting their mobile phone on silent. Relationships take time to build, and when each person invests more time in the other, their results will be great.

Businesspersons who interact with many clients will have to engage in much conversation, but they must make sure to set aside some time for their companion. If they work during the day, they can avoid taking too many calls in the evening. They can also set aside time on weekends for their companion, since they may be occupied during the week.

Those who fail to allocate quality time to communicate with their companions may find other persons invading their relationship and spending time talking to their partner. At the beginning, it may be tough not to accept every call, but it may be the best thing you can do to make more time for your companion.

15.3 Talk more with your companion

Each person must be intentional about talking more with their companion. While both persons may not like to engage in much conversation, it is important that at least one of them enjoy talking. When both persons in the relationship are silent, they may not spend time getting to know each other or doing things to make their relationship grow. Over time, partners may begin to feel like strangers in the relationship.

16. Minimize busyness

When persons are in love, they must make time for each other. While they may have been busy before they started their relationship, they have to adjust their activities to allocate more time for their partner. A desire to have a romantic life will not be possible if both persons are too busy.

When two persons agree to be involved in a relationship, they must be willing to readjust some of their routine activities. On many occasions, both persons may be studying or engaged in business. This may only be for a period of time, and when that time is over, they will have more time for themselves.

If persons want to accomplish certain things, then it is important that they occupy themselves with the things that bring them great success. But they must not allow themselves to be continuously overwhelmed by their activities.

Within some homes, one partner may choose to work while the other stays at home with the children. As the children grow from toddlers to adolescents, the parent who is working may end up working more in order to meet the financial needs of the family. This busyness by one parent may cause the partner who is at home to become more tired due to domestic activities. The partner who is working may find him or herself working longer hours or maybe even two jobs in order to provide more for the family. By the time some couples recognize it, they have spent five or ten years busy working to meet the needs of their children, and they have not taken any vacation or found much time for each other.

Parenting is a very demanding job, and it sometimes causes parents to be consumed with activities for the children and spend less time with their partner. It is always hoped that children will remember the sacrifices of their parents. Children must make their parents proud with their schoolwork and their involvement in domestic activities.

Parents must train their children at an early age to take part in domestic activities. When children know how to help out around the house, it will often give the parents more time to relax or to give more attention to each other.

When parents are busy with schoolwork and assisting in preparing meals for the children, they are often tired. These activities may continue for many years, until their children are working.

Section D. Relaxation and investment in your partner

Relaxation is important for every couple. Couples must carefully plan their vacations together so that they get time to learn more about each other. They can visit places they have never gone to before, which will be exciting for them. Some of these places will be within their own country, so they will get to learn more about it. Taking vacations in other countries is also important for couples to do.

Investing time and money in each partner can add to the quality of the relationship. Time must be set aside to interact with the children, but also for partners to talk with each other and share ideas. Couples may also set aside time to visit and interact with family members outside the household, which will allow them to learn more about their partner's background, and then they will know the things they should and should not do to their partner.

The theater may be a good place for couples to strengthen their romantic life. At the theater, they will watch plays that will make them smile and laugh. When couples are at home, they can watch family movies or series that will give them more insight into romance. When some couples first come together, they may not be aware of some of the things that will enhance their romantic life, but the movies will give them some important ideas that they can soon practice.

Celebrating birthdays and anniversaries helps couples to show more appreciation for each other. When they are celebrating these events, they can invite friends and relatives to join them.

The bedroom is a private place for couples. Therefore, not everyone must be allowed to visit a couple's bedroom. If the bedroom and bed are welcoming, then great things will happen in the bedroom for each partner. So, they must invest in their bedroom and have a happy romantic relationship.

17. Invest in your partner

When a person finds a partner, they must be intentional about investing in their partner, as this investment will work for their own benefit as well. Not everyone will come from wealthy homes, but if someone has enough funds, then it will be a great decision to use some of that money to invest in their partner.

17.1 Time

One of the resources that some relationships are lacking is time. They fail to invest time in each other, and that may be the reason why so many relationships struggle. While both persons may be busy with so many activities, they must set aside time for their partner. The romantic relationship will grow when they spend time together, support each other, eat together, and sleep together.

For example, some wives are too busy looking after the children. When they finish with the children, then they are busy with other domestic activities. Some men are too busy trying to earn money to take care of the family, and others are too occupied with cleaning the vehicle or spending time with their friends. Both partners must sacrifice their time to be with each other.

When couples spend too much time with their children, they will leave little time for each other. These children will grow into adults and soon have their own families, and their parents will not have spent enough time learning about and loving each other, since they were too busy attending to the children.

17.2 Money

Apart from time, couples must invest financially in each other. If both partners are working, they may decide who is to pay the major bills and who may invest their money. They may set aside money for savings and for investment in their education.

Money should also be set aside for partners to invest in each other. While they may not each be able to invest the same value, they may be able to do something with their contribution that will delight their partner. Sometimes, it is not the value of the gifts that matters, but the sentiment that goes into the gifts.

If one partner is at home attending to the children, then the other partner must show appreciation for them. If one partner has to work daily, then the partner who is at home must also show some appreciation and invest in their companion.

On birthdays and other special dates, one partner may invest greatly in their companion. However, they must not wait for those special days, but invest in each other as often as possible. Regular investments in a partner may work in the investor's favor, so make your partner feel appreciated by investing in them now, rather than later.

18. Vacation

Couples can become tired of being at home. When couples are living together, it is not a prison for them, but they still need to find some time to be away from home and see other places.

New places may create an opportunity for couples to think of many great things. They may have more time to talk about their disagreements and how they can fix their own problems. Every couple will experience problems, but if they do not find ways of fixing those problems, they will soon find many more things going in the wrong direction.

Couples who attend counseling sessions may be advised to arrange a vacation and get some alone time. This may be difficult at first, as they think of the many things they may not be able to complete at home. However, if they really need to build their relationship, then they have to invest in themselves.

Couples can arrange a vacation at least once a year or some longer timespan. The vacation can include their children, but couples must also think of themselves and stop putting everything and everyone else above them. Even from one vacation, some couples will probably rekindle their relationship. Their relationship will increase in value as each partner learns to appreciate the other. Building a romantic relationship will take time and money, but it is a worthwhile investment.

18.1 Location and cost

When couples are considering a vacation, they must think of the cost that they plan to incur. They must also consider locations that are most suitable for them and make a final decision as to where they will go. For couples who go on regular vacations together, they may choose a different location each time, since they see their vacations as another opportunity to learn about new places and people.

Couples can decide if they want indoor or outdoor locations. Some couples spend most of their time indoors, and they are glad to take a vacation where they will enjoy nature. They may go to some fun parks or go hiking. Wherever they go and whatever they plan to do, they must have fun and return with more energy to rekindle their relationship.

Within many countries, couples will have a number of places where they can go for vacation, some of which may be within driving distance. Persons often have not explored many of the tourist sites in their own country. Perhaps they have not gone on vacation within their own country, but have gone to vacation destinations in many other countries.

19. Time with children and relatives

When couples are together, it does not mean that they must isolate themselves from everyone else. There are some persons who are only concerned about their relationship, perhaps not even making an effort to see their companion's relatives. They will spend most of their time at home or at work, but not venture out to connect with other relatives.

19.1 Spending time with children

Couples who have children must spend time with them. There are some games that the entire family can participate in, including indoor board games like Scrabble and chess.

Families can play fun sports like table tennis and lawn tennis together, which will often allow them to bond. On many occasions, as the family has fun together, children learn more about their parents and parents learn more about their children.

When some couples plan vacations, it is for the entire family. This can be a great opportunity for children to see different places.

As parents spend time with their children, they may get them to be more involved in domestic activities. For example, parents can teach their children to cook or clean the house. On the first few occasions, some children will not do a good job, but with constant help from their parents, they will improve.

As parents build their relationship with each other, they must not forget their children. When children see parents working as a team, it often causes them to bond together and love their parents.

19.2 Interacting with family members

Couples must set aside time to interact with their relatives. This may require the husband to go with his wife to visit her parents, or the wife to go with her husband to see his family. With these constant interactions and visits, each partner may grow and appreciate each other more.

When some persons learn more about their companion's background, it may cause them to have great respect for their companion. For example, knowing that their companion came from a single-parent home may cause someone to show more love to their companion, who was not accustomed to being loved by both parents when they were at home with their single parent.

Many times when a person enters a relationship, they are looking for the things that were missing from their earlier days, while others would like to continue the things they saw their parents doing. This may include working as a team, validating each other, or spending time dancing.

Whenever a person enters a relationship, they are expecting life to be better for them. Therefore, each companion must create a safe space where their partner does not regret choosing them. Most persons are looking to have progress in their relationship, so every relationship must provide opportunities for each person to learn and grow with the other. While they will have challenges, their days of happiness must be greater than their days of problems.

20. Movies and theaters

Couples should take the time to go to the theater together. While there may be individual plays that each person would like to see, they must make a deliberate attempt to find plays that they will both benefit from. At the theater, they can eat together, hold hands, and do many things that will build their relationship. While these events may be small, they can lead to many things that will enhance the romance in the relationship.

At the theater, they may be eating from the same container, or they may share a meal with each other. For example, if they purchase popcorn or other snacks, they may take turns feeding each other, which may be a fun activity that draws them closer to each other.

At the theater, one partner may fall asleep in the safe arms of their companion. One partner may go to the theater just to please their companion, and this is acceptable in relationships, since persons may have to do things that bring happiness to their companion.

If couples have their own vehicles, one partner may drive from home to the theater and the other partner may drive on the way back. Some couples take turns sponsoring the night at the theater, where one partner will pay to enter the theater and the other will purchase the snacks and beverages. There are other occasions where one partner will pay for everything, and the next time, the other partner will do likewise.

20.1 Watching movies

Whether couples watch movies at home or at the cinema, they can choose movies that will help them to enhance their romantic life. When some persons get into a relationship, they may be very intelligent, but not too familiar with what they need to do in a relationship. As they both watch the movies they have selected, they will learn many important things that will boost their love-making life.

There are some romantic movies, perhaps by a particular director, that often have good storylines. These movies may highlight specific things that new couples may find very interesting. There are also some television series that are important teaching materials for persons who need guidance with their romantic life. As a couple sets aside time in the evening or weekends to watch movies, either partner can decide what they want to watch.

No one is born with the full knowledge of how to be good with romance. In some homes, parents might have had much conflict, so that is what their children learn in terms of relationships. So, when those children are adults and take companions, they are not aware of how to treat them. However, after watching certain movies and practicing some of the things they have learned, they become better with romance. When persons learn more about romance and put those tips to practical use, their relationship may soon become more enjoyable, and their companion may be delighted about the decision to choose them. A relationship without romance will lead to many conflicts, which may result in both persons making unhealthy decisions.

21. Sports and entertainment

Too many couples are stuck at the office, at home, or at religious institutions. It is time to for them to roll up their sleeves and get involved in the game. They must have fun together. They must learn how to compete against each other, to win, and then to still remain as a family.

Sports often brings out competitiveness in people. When couples compete, they get an understanding of each other's thinking and strategies. Some sports will require a great deal of strength, and participants must be willing to show that strength. There are other sports that require much critical thinking.

As couples compete in sports, it gives them more opportunity for physical contact, which may further stimulate their interest in each other. When couples avoid physical contact, they rob themselves of an opportunity to enhance the romance in their life together.

Many outdoor sports will allow persons to burn energy and be fit. If they are very active in sports, they may not have to visit the gym very often, since they have found another way of exercising.

For some sports, the husband and wife may be on different teams, so they will have to compete against each other. There are other sports where the husband and wife will be on the same team, so they will agree on the same direction to compete and win. Some families may include their children in the sports, which will increase the competition among the entire family.

If someone has an anger problem, they may not like to compete and lose. However, as they participate in family sports, that anger may subside, and they may become a more understanding and patient person.

If the sport requires the wife to climb a mountain, tree, or wall, she may need her husband to lift her to the point where she can begin to maneuver by herself. If a husband is running a marathon and needs water along the way, his wife may be there to provide it for him. These actions may make one partner appreciate the love and support given to them by their companion.

In lawn tennis, both partners can compete in the doubles competition. They can play these matches among family members and friends, since many couples may not be professionally trained to be competitive in this sport. But through the mere fact that they are playing as a team and on the same side, they may become more connected and find joy in supporting each other.

There are some sports that couples can play at the beach, such as beach volleyball. Couples can also play some sports in the pool, though it must be shallow for those who do not know how to swim. After a joint engagement, once the couple finishes playing, they can go swimming or sit in the water and relax. Being in water often feels refreshing, and when couples enjoy this activity, they may be more relaxed to discuss certain aspects of their relationship.

22. Allocate funds for family entertainment

Many couples work very hard and spend most of their money on external things. Their sense of accomplishment is in their material possessions, and they do not give much attention to their companion.

Figure 9. Things that couples prioritize above family entertainment

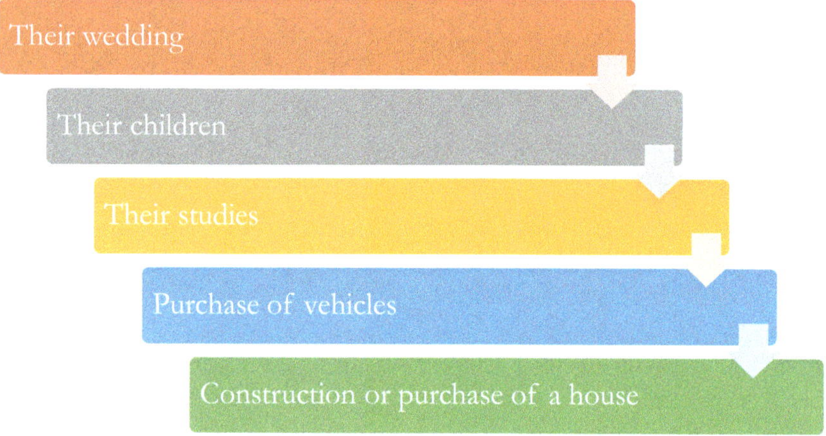

For some families, this list can be even longer. However, the problem is that little or no money is allocated for family entertainment. It is no surprise that many relationships suffer because neither partner has considered setting money aside for entertainment. When children grow older, they will spend less time with their parents, so family entertainment is important now.

The amount of money that couples invest to acquire a vehicle or house is great, yet they fail to set aside even a small portion of their funds for entertainment. It has been seen over and over that before some persons have finished paying for their vehicles and houses, one partner may become sick or even die, and they did not take the opportunity for entertainment and quality time together.

Many forms of entertainment can be arranged to meet any budget. Most times, both persons are aware of the money they have remaining, so they know how much they can spend on entertainment. When couples spend money on entertainment, they will be building their relationship, and instead of having regular disagreements, they will have more fun time together. Families can entertain themselves right at home. Sometimes, it is the simple things people do that create great value in the relationship. Couples must avoid seeking loans to finance their entertainment, since after the entertainment is over, they will have debts to settle.

23. Celebrating anniversaries

Celebrating birthdays and wedding anniversaries is good for couples to do, as they must be thankful for life. Many persons do not recognize that it is by the saving grace of the Creator that they have had life for another 365 days. There are often many deaths during each year, and many persons are affected by accidents. So, when it comes to anniversaries, celebrate these important dates.

Some husbands and wives will go on vacation for their birthdays or wedding anniversaries. They do this because they want a moment to relax and just spend time with each other. Many partners do not recognize that the stresses of life sometimes cause them to have disagreements. However, they must find reasons to celebrate each other and to celebrate important dates in their lives.

If couples want to go someplace where they can have privacy for their wedding anniversaries, then they must do so. After all, they must find ways of fostering their relationship. When couples have children, they sometimes do not have much privacy and may not have enough time for each other. However, when they have a moment to celebrate, they must capitalize on that important moment.

When relationships are going through difficulties, it is important for couples to spend some time away from the presence of others and reflect on their relationship. They must discuss why they both decided to get together in the first place. As they discuss their initial days of falling in love, it may cause them to appreciate their companion and put their differences aside.

For birthday celebrations, either partner can choose to sponsor or surprise their companion. This is a good thing to do, as some partners are waiting the whole year to be surprised and celebrated. These anniversary celebrations can be hosted at home or at another location, which gives couples much time to celebrate.

Figure 10. Important things for couples' anniversary celebrations

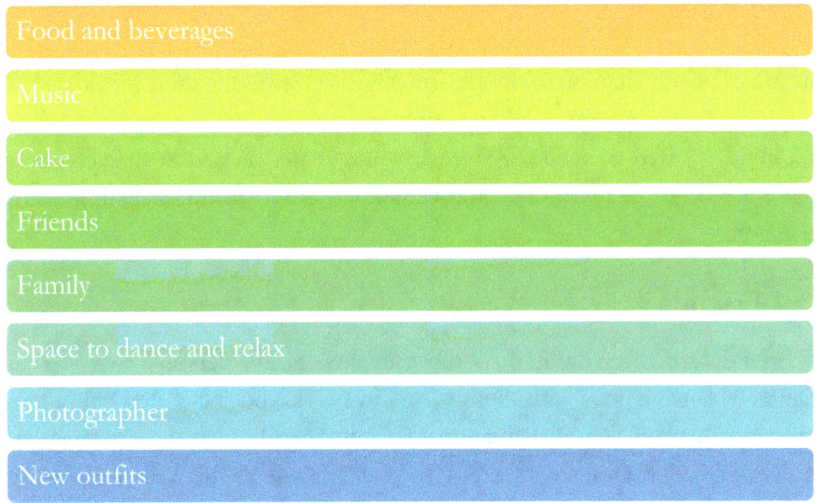

23.1 Food and beverages

At these important celebrations, couples are happy to eat together. Food and beverages will be provided for the couple, their friends and family, and other special invitees. When persons eat together at these anniversaries, they often share many important memories and may bring laughter to those who are celebrating.

Different persons may prefer different foods and beverages, so those who are inviting others to a celebration must consider their audience's preference. Oftentimes, there will be both alcoholic and non-alcoholic drinks at these celebrations.

23.2 Music

Music is something that many persons like to have for their birthday and anniversary celebrations. The music may be soothing to the ears of those who are celebrating. Persons who like the songs and know how to sing may decide to sing along.

There may be persons who want to sing for the one who is celebrating their birthday or anniversary. Some persons are blessed with good singing voices, and they will make everyone happy to hear them.

23.3 Cake

At many birthday celebrations, a cake is one of the important things that will be placed on the table. There is much fun and laughter when it is time to cut the cake and share with the person who is celebrating their birthday. For couples celebrating their wedding anniversary, there may be much laughter, and invitees often want to see them kiss and share the cake with each other. There are often many phones and cameras there to capture this important moment.

23.4 Friends

Friends are often invited to these events. Some persons have certain friends who have been with them for many years, and they often enjoy each other's company. The participation of friends tends to make birthday and anniversary celebrations very happy, as they are able to share their memories of past experiences, both good and bad. Friends may share well wishes and greetings with those who are celebrating.

23.5 Family

Family members are important persons to invite to birthday and anniversary celebrations. As a matter of fact, sometimes they are the ones who organize these celebrations. Relatives may contribute to the celebrations in different ways. For example, one family member may volunteer to be the MC for the event. Other family members may choose to stay at home and look after the younger children and babies. Persons must not ignore their families, as they may need them when everyone else has rejected them.

23.6 Space to dance and relax

For some persons, birthday and anniversary celebrations will not be complete without dancing. In the case of wedding anniversaries, couples may have to dance for the benefit of the invitees. One partner may be shy, but they may dance anyway to please the invitees. No one expects perfect dancing from the couples; they just want them to have fun. Many persons may be waiting for the music to start so that they can have some fun dancing. Couples who like to dance may be the ones to start off the dancing session.

When persons organize birthday and wedding celebrations, they must ensure that there are tables and chairs for the attendees to relax while they eat and drink. After persons have eaten, then it may be time to dance and have fun.

23.7 Photographer

When photographs are taken, it allows persons to reflect on past events. Some couples may hire a professional photographer to attend their wedding anniversary and take photographs for them, which they will keep in their album or circulate electronically.

Many couples still have photographs from their wedding day. They will then add each year's anniversary photographs to the previous set so they can reflect on their years of togetherness.

23.8 New outfits

Some persons choose to wear a great new outfit to their birthday or wedding anniversary celebrations. Sometimes, the outfit gets everyone talking about how good it fits that person. They may not be bothered about how much the outfit cost them, since they want to look special for that day.

When couples are celebrating together, they may both wear the same outfit, with shoes in matching colors. Since they know that it is their special day, they will do everything necessary to make it a great day for them.

24. The couple's bedroom and bed

One great investment that couples must make is to ensure that their bedroom makes them feel comfortable and relaxed. Their bed must welcome them every time they lie down on it.

Many couples spend long hours working and few hours resting. However, the short time they spend in bed must account for the hard work and stressful day they have had.

24.1 Separate bed for children

When parents have newborn babies, they may want to spend a lot of time with them, so they may allow the babies to sleep in the same bed with them, or in the same room with a separate bed. However, once the babies are old enough to be placed in their own rooms, then couples must do that as early as possible.

24.2 The bedroom is off limits to many persons

The bedrooms for couples must be off limits to others. Children must know that they cannot invade their parents' room whenever they feel like it. There are some couples who will invite family members and friends to their bedrooms. However, these visitors should be kept in the outer part of the house, as the bedroom must be seen as a private place for couples and not a meeting place for many persons.

24.3 Beautiful fragrance in the bedroom

Having a sweet-smelling fragrance in the bedroom will lighten the nostrils of both partners and make them want to get closer to each other. Oftentimes, the fragrance puts their minds at ease and gives them more time to think of each other.

Some couples have a preferred fragrance that they will use in the bedroom, which is different from the fragrance used in other parts of the house. Some men will allow their female companion to shop for the fragrance, since she may have her own preference. In cases where the husband is at better at purchasing fragrances, then the wife should allow him to make this purchase.

24.4 Special lighting for the bedroom

The lighting in the bedroom often is not as bright as the external security light of the property. The light effect can be very conducive for couples.

24.5 Bedsheet and bed cover

As small a matter as it may seem, the sheet and cover on the bed may have a great impact on romance. The color and material of the sheets can be motivating for couples. While couples may not say too much when they are alone in the bedroom, the smallest thing can be a distraction and must be avoided by both partners. After some years of togetherness, each person must try and understand their partner and make their relationship even better.

If the mood is right and the bedroom is welcoming, many great things will happen for a couple. Enjoy your relationship and keep building your romantic life.

Reference List

Tull, A., & Coward, A. (2009). *Caribbean food and nutrition for CSEC*. Oxford University Press.

About the Author

Author Geary Reid wants to see more couples enjoy their romantic life. When couples love each other and invest in their romance, they keep intruders away from their relationships.

Over the years, Geary Reid has heard so many complaints from persons saying that their romantic life is dead. In his discussions with some persons, he has seen that it is the simple things they were not doing that caused their relationship to fall apart. However, Reid offers hope to many couples that they can begin to express their emotions to each other in so many different ways, and they must start now.

Reid likes to see couples dancing together, as it allows them to embrace each other. When couples participate in sports, they burn energy, but more importantly, they have more opportunities to touch and hold each other, which can set the stage for romance. When couples dine together, it can be a starting point for their romantic relationship, as they can once again hold each other's hands, feed each other, and dance to songs that make them feel happy about their partner.

With over two decades of married life, Geary Reid shares some of the things he's learned, things he's heard other couples discuss, and many things he sees happening daily among couples. He believes that if more persons are willing to show their emotion to their companions, there will be more romance in their relationships and they will have less time for arguments. Sometimes, one partner longs to be very close with the other, but the children occupy too much of their partner's time. Reid believes couples must not invite everyone into their bedroom but instead keep it for themselves. When the bedroom is attractive, couples often spend more time together there.

Persons sometimes forget to celebrate their partner's birthday, which may cause offense. Some couples have not put much emphasis on celebrating wedding anniversaries and other important things, and when their relationships begin to experience problems, they wonder how this could have happened. However, Geary Reid is encouraging everyone to look for every opportunity to acknowledge and celebrate with their companion. These celebrations will draw couples closer to each other.

This page is intentionally left blank.